HAYNES EXPLAINS
TEENAGERS

Owners' Workshop Manual

© Haynes Publishing • Written by **Boris Starling**

Published in October 2016
Reprinted in July 2017

A catalogue record for this book is available from the British Library

ISBN 978 1 78521 103 4

Haynes Publishing, Sparkford, Yeovil,
Somerset BA22 7JJ, UK
Tel: +44 (0) 1963 440635
Website: www.haynes.com

Haynes North America, Inc.,
861 Lawrence Drive, Newbury Park,
California 91320, USA

Printed and bound in Malaysia

Cover image from Getty Images

Written by **Boris Starling**
Edited by **Louise McIntyre**
Designed by **Richard Parsons**

Safety first!

Teenagers are in general both temperamental and unhygienic, so it is imperative that you take appropriate precautions before approaching them. The Teenage habit of listening to music through headphones at a volume which makes pneumatic drills sound like birdsong means they can be easily startled, which in turn leads to sulking. Stand in their eyeline and ensure they are aware of your presence before proceeding. Do not enter their rooms without first donning rubber gloves and appropriate anti-bacterial shoe covers.

Working facilities

Optimal working space for Teenagers depends on the identity of those with whom they're obliged to share it. If only other Teenagers are present (particularly attractive ones – see The horn, page 26), they usually need less than $1m^2$ per person. If even a single adult is present, however, Teenagers prefer a minimum of $1km^2$. Given the state of Teenage hygiene (see above), however, this Chernobyl-style exclusion zone is a stipulation that many adults will think entirely reasonable, if not even a little conservative.

Contents

Introduction

Welcome to *Haynes Explains: Teenagers*. This book is for you if you are thinking of having a Teenager, or if you have a Teenager at the moment. If you've already had a Teenager and have survived intact, you probably won't want to revisit the experience in this world or the next.

Perhaps a more accurate title would be *Haynes Tries Our Best To Explain: Teenagers*. You may wish to hum the *Mission: Impossible* theme while reading this. We certainly did while writing it. Of all models covered in this series, Teenagers are by far the most unreliable, temperamental and highly strung.

They are 1970s Alfa Romeo Alfasud Sprints in a world of 21st-century Skoda diesels. They are 1960s Soviet motorbikes in a world of Honda Fireblades. They are any vehicle made in a French factory on a Friday afternoon in a world of ruthless German micro-precision.

What Teenagers think is not what they say; what they say is not what they do. One moment Teenagers are zipping along happy and carefree; the next they are slewed across the hard shoulder refusing to move and resistant to the best efforts of the RAC (Rejected Adults' Confederation).

About this manual

The aim of this manual is to help you get the best value from your Teenager. It can do this in several ways. It can help you (a) decide what work must be done (b) tackle this work yourself, though you may choose to have much of it performed by an off-site garage such as a boarding school and/or Young Offenders' Institution.

The manual has drawings and descriptions to show the function and layout of the various components.

Tasks are described in a logical order so that even a novice can do the work, which should prove useful to those whose brains have been turned to porridge by the relentless demands of getting children to the age of 12 years and 364 days. We would like to tell you that the hard part is over, but like George Washington we cannot tell a lie. In the words of those three great sages Bachman, Turner and Overdrive, you ain't seen nothing yet.

Dimensions, weights and capacities

Overall height (average, 13–19 years)

Teenager XY	140–190cm
Teenager XX	135–175cm

Both models may grow 10cm in as many minutes during egregious growth spurt.

Kerb weight (average, 13–19 years)

Teenager XY	45–70kg
Teenager XX	45–58kg

Capacities

For argument	bottomless
For interpersonal drama	you just don't understand
For alcohol	less than they think

Intervals between refuelling

Night-time	9 hours
Daytime	9 minutes

Maximum speed and acceleration

First thing in morning	1.5mph. 0–maximum: 45 mins
When angry	7434mph. 0–60: 0.000005 sec

Engine

Bore	that's what grown-ups are for
Stroke	suppressed giggling 'you said stroke'
Power	168bhp ('but he PROMISED'
	rather than 'brake horsepower')
Torque	278lb ft (where objects being twisted
	= words. HE SAID THAT HE DID)
Redline	oh yes. Very easy to access

Electrical issues

Haynes Explains: Babies covered the rewiring which occurs in the brains of small children as they become accustomed to the world. A similar rewiring takes place in Teenagers, and this time it's much worse. Teenagers are larger, they use many more swear words, and they're much harder to handle.

A schematic of the Teenager's brain looks like an explosion in a spaghetti factory or the Los Angeles highway system from the air.

The frontal lobes in the Teenager's brain, which control impulses, reasoning and planning, are the last to be rewired for adulthood. While the electricians are in they reroute decision-making through the amygdala, which is long on threats and short on insight and empathy. So Teenagers are literally not all there. They love to be reminded of this.

⚠ The extent of the rewiring

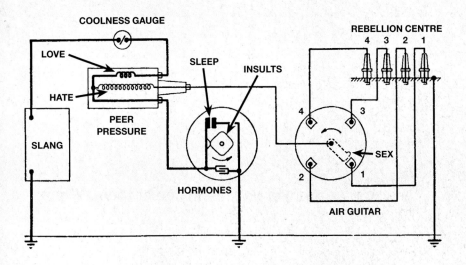

FIG 2•1 **THE EXTENT OF THE TEENAGERS' REWIRING**

⚠ Babies vs Teenagers

The contrast between Babies and Teenagers demonstrates the extent of this rewiring. Where Babies involve you in every decision they make – choice of breakfast cereal, first visit to the toilet, choice of T-shirt, second visit to the toilet, which way round the park to go, third visit to the toilet – Teenagers exclude you from as much as possible.

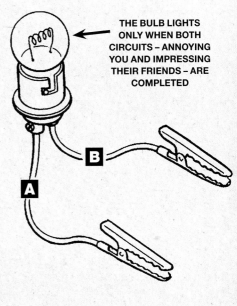

THE BULB LIGHTS ONLY WHEN BOTH CIRCUITS – ANNOYING YOU AND IMPRESSING THEIR FRIENDS – ARE COMPLETED

FIG 2•2 **LIGHTBULB MOMENT**

1) Babies want to have babies themselves and never leave home. Teenagers vow to remain child-free forever as they think children are 'too much like hard work' and 'offer little return on investment'. (If you keep a straight face when they say this, consider a career in poker).

2) Babies like their bedroom doors open so they know where you are day and night. A Teenager's bedroom door is more firmly closed than a cell at the Scrubs.

3) Babies treat life as a happy family comedy. Teenagers treat life as a Cold War spy movie, and the enemy is you. You know their name, date of birth, class year and mobile phone number. Anything else is on a need-to-know basis, and you don't need to know it.

When you have Babies, your friends come round and coo at them. When you have Teenagers, your friends send you sad-face texts saying 'thoughts and prayers are with you'.

7

Jump-starting

Teenagers are notoriously unreliable before 8am and after 8pm. In order to get going, vehicles in the olden days used a valve to modify the air pressure in the intake manifold and alter the ratio of fuel and air entering the engine. This was called a choke. You may feel the same way about your Teenager.

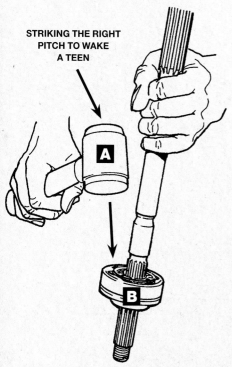

STRIKING THE RIGHT
PITCH TO WAKE
A TEEN

FIG 2•3 **STRIKING THE RIGHT PITCH**

Morning
Getting Teenagers to wake up is like disturbing a hibernating bear, except the bear is more reasonable about it. Teenagers have trouble starting on cold mornings, warm mornings, wet mornings, light mornings, dark mornings and all mornings on days with a 'Y' in their name.

Teenagers need nine hours of sleep per night, but biological patterns mean they find it hard to drift off before 11pm. Hence they will still need more sleep when you're getting them up for school. This is a mismatch between the demands of biology and those of the Department of Education.

Night
The nocturnal Teenager proves their knowledge of algebra with the equation **Th = Ta + 120 (PR x STW)**, where:

Th	The time they arrive home
Ta	The time they agreed to come home
120	Number of minutes elapsed
PR	Parental Rage
STW	Shrugged Teenage Whatevs

⚠ How to wake a teenager...

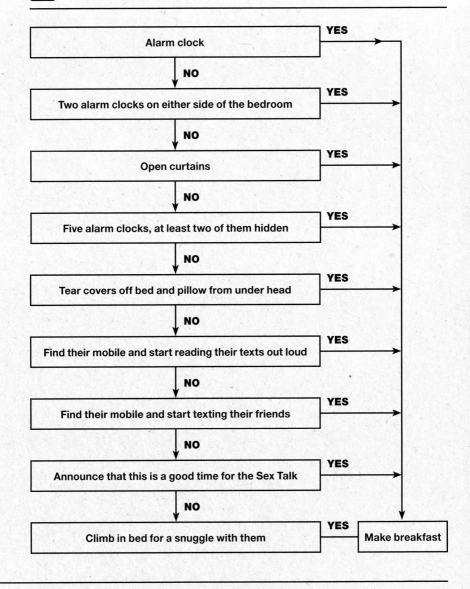

Controls

Teenagers have two pedals, an accelerator and a brake. The extent to which the accelerator is engaged is directly proportional to the stupidity of the anticipated course of action. When Teenagers are considering doing something especially moronic, which might involve being egged on by their imbecilic friends, a temporary turboboost function kicks in.

Teenagers never use the front or side repeaters, because indicating to others what you intend to do is really uncool and strictly for squares.

The brake does not work. Never has, never will. The Teenage handbrake, on the other hand, does come into play. Judicious application of the handbrake allows a 180-degree turn, which in turn permits the Teenager to deny something that has literally just happened and change their mind from one moment to the next. Plus handbrakes are wicked for doing doughnuts in supermarket car parks at 2am.

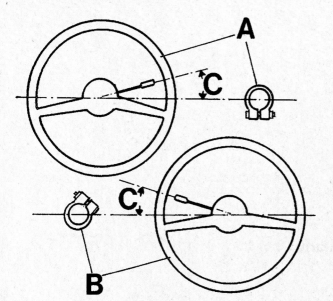

A EQUILIBRIUM. STEERING A SENSIBLE COURSE

B INNOCUOUS SUGGESTION WHICH THREATENS SAID COURSE

C DIVERSION. ONLY A SMALL AMOUNT, BUT STILL LEADS TO DISASTER

FIG 2•4 **STAYING ON THE STRAIGHT AND NARROW**

The teenage gearbox

The Teenager's gearbox is automatic
and can shift between gears

a) apparently at random
b) faster than Porsche's
Doppelkupplungsgetriebe,
one of the most advanced
dual-clutch transmissions
available today.

Six forward gears:
1) This Is The Best
Thing Ever
2) But Everyone Else
Has Got One
3) Leave Me Alone
4) I Hate You
5) Of Course Nothing's
Going To Go Wrong
6) I Don't Even Fancy Them
Anyway So Shut Up

and two reverse ones:
1) My Life Is Over
2) OK, I Did Do It But
I Didn't Mean To.

**Under particularly
rapid downshifting,
a high-pitched
'it's so unfair' can
sometimes be heard.**

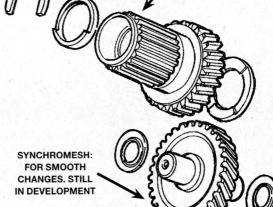

LOW-RANGE TRANSFER:
FOR DIFFICULT CONDITIONS.
STANDARD

SYNCHROMESH:
FOR SMOOTH
CHANGES. STILL
IN DEVELOPMENT

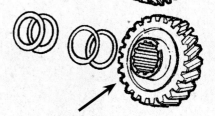

OVERDRIVE: FOR
ECONOMIC CRUISING.
RARELY USED

FIG 2·5 **TRANSMISSION:
IMPOSSIBLE TEENAGERS**

11

Sound system

There are two possible reasons why you hate the Teenager's music:

1) As people get older, their ability to distinguish between consonant and dissonant sounds diminishes, meaning they engage less with music.

2) Teenage music is rubbish and it was much better in your day.

The second is always true.
You hate Teenagers' music just as your parents hated your music when you were a Teenager, and so on.

FIG 2•6 **EARACHE – WHEN THE KILOHERTZ HURTS**

⚠ Discussion topics

Select **TWO** of the following topics for discussion with your Teenager.

a) Why's he wearing all that make-up? Does he have a skin problem?

b) Is that a boy or a girl? We had all this with Boy George, you know.

c) You can't even hear what he's singing. He'd probably have a nice voice if he stopped screeching.

d) I do like that **[INSERT NAME OF POPULAR MALE SINGER]**. He seems a nice young man.

e) And that Taylor Swift. Very catchy tunes. It's her real name, you know.

f) All these talent shows aren't real music. It's just bland, overmarketed autotuned pap. Why can't you listen to proper rebellious music?

⚠ Perpetual motion

For centuries, scientists have been trying to make perpetual motion machines but have always failed – until now. Harnessing the energy exchanged between Teenager and parent over the ideal volume for music could revolutionise technology as we know it.

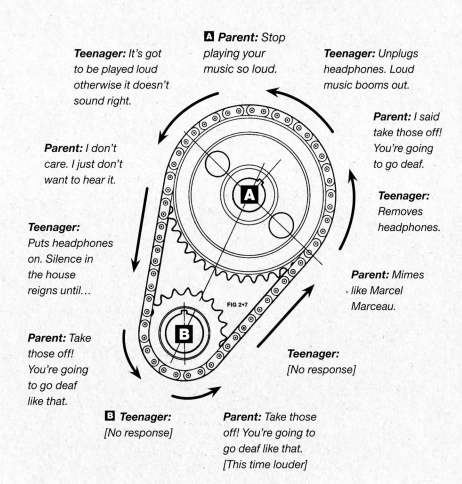

A *Parent:* Stop playing your music so loud.

Teenager: It's got to be played loud otherwise it doesn't sound right.

Parent: I don't care. I just don't want to hear it.

Teenager: Puts headphones on. Silence in the house reigns until…

Parent: Take those off! You're going to go deaf like that.

B *Teenager:* [No response]

Parent: Take those off! You're going to go deaf like that. [This time louder]

Teenager: [No response]

Parent: Mimes like Marcel Marceau.

Teenager: Removes headphones.

Parent: I said take those off! You're going to go deaf.

Teenager: Unplugs headphones. Loud music booms out.

FIG 2•7

Bodykits and accessorising

Whenever you are in the same place as your Teenager, there are seven words guaranteed to start World War Three: **'you're not going out dressed like that.'**

Teenagers' dress sense moves quicker than Usain Bolt, so *Haynes Explains* will not attempt any specific advice. Take jeans, for example. One moment ripped and torn, then bleach-washed, stonewashed (rarely just normally washed if the Teenager has anything to do with it), distressed (as you will be when you see the price tag), boot cut, wide leg, low rise, skinny, baggy, and back to ripped.

There's one thing Teenagers want more than looking good, and that's not looking foolish. They dress the same way to fit in.

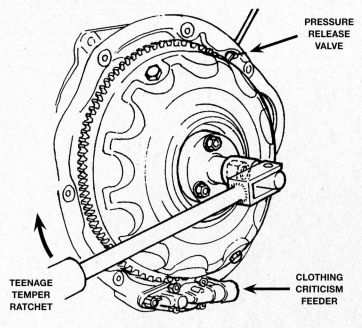

PRESSURE
RELEASE
VALVE

TEENAGE
TEMPER
RATCHET

CLOTHING
CRITICISM
FEEDER

FIG 2•8 **THE TEENAGER WIND-UP MACHINE**

⚠ Chromosome XX and XY

There are major differences between the way Female Teenagers (chromosome XX) and Male Teenagers (chromosome XY) like to dress:

Teenager XX

Like to experiment. They hang out in shops for hours on end, irritate the staff by trying on outfits they can't afford, take photos in the changing rooms of themselves in said outfits and upload said photos to social media.

They bond over the minutiae of the ensemble: long necklaces or short? High-waisted shorts or skinny jeans? Converse or vintage shoes? Teenager XX fashion time is like an endless mix-and-match from children's books. If you are a mother, you may find it especially annoying that your Teenager XX can fit into jeans that have been too skinny for you ever since – and as a direct result of – giving birth to her.

Teenager XY

Give as little thought to their outfit as possible, or at least that's what they like you to think. They get attached to certain items in the wardrobe and wear them incessantly. They will never voluntarily wash their clothes: their clothes, in fact, often get up and walk to the washing machine themselves to commit Persil hara-kiri.

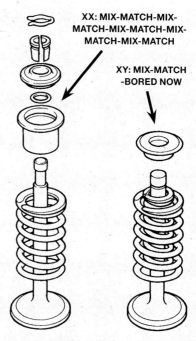

XX: MIX-MATCH-MIX-MATCH-MIX-MATCH-MIX-MATCH-MIX-MATCH

XY: MIX-MATCH -BORED NOW

FIG 2•9 **DIFFERENCES IN XX AND XY**

Many Teenagers like to adorn themselves with accessories in metal and ink. It is best if you can persuade them to ensure that the metal ones are removable and the ink ones concealable.

Service history

Mechanics and engineers are required to submit service reports on Teenagers at least three times a year. Many engineers resent this (as do many more Teenagers): they have many Teenagers to monitor and don't like spending hours detailing said Teenagers' manifold shortcomings.

But nor do they want to lose their jobs, because at least they get paid for taking the Teenagers off your hands for five days a week. As a result, they often write the service reports in code, making things look brighter than they are.

Beware the Teenager who comes without a full service history. Teenagers may claim that their service reports have been turned to pulp in a car wash, or are even as they speak progressing through a canine alimentary canal, or have been carried away by a tornado. Such Teenagers may flunk school but will probably end up making a fortune in Hollywood.

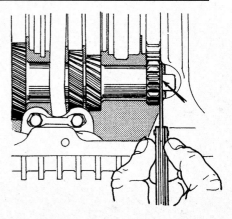

FIG 2•10 **TWEAKING THE SERVICE HISTORY**

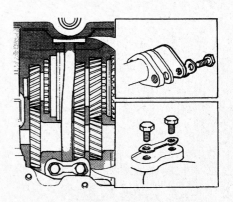

FIG 2•11 **A VERY DELICATE JOB**

Teenagers care very much what their reports say, though as usual they would no more admit this than fly to the moon.

⚠ Understanding your school report

What the report says	What the report means
Independent	Disobedient
Animated	Disruptive
Informal	Cheeky
Expressive	Complains
Intense	Thank God we don't have guns here
Inquisitive	Keeps breaching Internet firewall
Relaxed	Bone idle
Has potential	Bone idle
Strong leadership skills	Atrociously bossy
Vivid imagination	Pathological liar
Likes to question and challenge	Know-it-all
Satisfactory progress	Deeply average
Good understanding of the rules	Tells tales incessantly
Must do neater work at school	Stop doing his homework for him
Needs encouragement	Needs a bomb under her chair
Expresses himself vividly	Swears like a docker
Works to a consistently high standard	You are pushy middle-class parents
Good at practical activities	Illiterate
Likes to do things his own way	Pig-headed
Willing to engage in discussion	Argumentative
Took a while to settle in	We didn't like each other
I wish her well next year	Thank God she won't be in my class
Surprisingly good exam result	Cheated
I look forward to a big improvement	I believe in fairies
RHINO	Really Here In Name Only

Connection problems

Even the most illiterate teenager is fluent in three languages: Teen English, Teen Pure and Text.

1. Teen English
This is more or less the language you're familiar with but rather economical with the truth. And yes – your Teenager speaks it just as much as any of their peers.

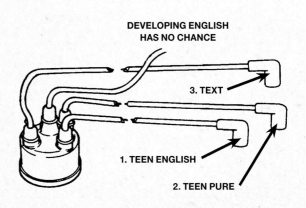

DEVELOPING ENGLISH HAS NO CHANCE

3. TEXT

1. TEEN ENGLISH

2. TEEN PURE

FIG 2•12 **TEENAGE CONNECTIONS**

2. Teen Pure
Teen Pure is a different kettle of fish requiring more thorough translation. To adult ears, Teen Pure is only slightly less incomprehensible than the whistling of the Clangers.

WARNING

Understanding Teen Pure does not give you licence to speak it. Do not speak it under any circumstances. It's like pronouncing 'Van Gogh' as 'Van Hoe' rather than 'Van Goff' – you may be technically right, but you'll sound like an idiot.

Below is an examples of typical sentences translated from English to Teen Pure.

Example 1:
English: Jamal's extremely attractive girlfriend was very angry with him when he chose to hang out with his friends rather than stay at home with her. She flew into a rage and stormed off. It was very funny.

Teen Pure: Jamal's proper buff missus was tampin' 'cos he wanted to jam with his bred'rins instead of chillaxing in her crib. She got like well lairy and legged it. It was bare jokes.

Understanding *Teen English*

Teen English	Real English
I cleaned my room	You can now see some of the floor
Can I have a couple of friends over?	A dozen people will be turning up at the front door round... about... now
I'm going to do homework in my room	I'm going to my room to spend three hours on social media
Can I go round to Ryan's? His parents are at home, definitely	Please don't call them to check
Of course I was nice to my sister	She ran away before I could hit her
She said I could borrow it	She might have done if I'd asked her
You said I could spend the weekend with them!	If I'm convincing enough, you might believe me

3. Text

Text speak looks more like a computer diagnostic of system failure than an actual language.

> **Hru?**
> **Gr8. Watchin TV wiv GOAT.**
> **CD9 POS.**
> **SMH. TTYL.**
> **U2.**

Didn't understand that? You're not supposed to. Text speak is like an episode of *Countdown* where someone's stolen half of Rachel Riley's letter cards. And that's before we get to the unholy mash-up of Egyptian hieroglyphics and toilet door icons which are emojis. Teenagers could write a novel the length of *War and Peace* using only emojis. There are more than 60 different emoji faces, representing everything from happiness to despair via anger, fretfulness, kissing and many others.

When lexicographers spoke of a world language, they meant something like Esperanto, not pictures of cupcakes and clapping hands.

The CPU

The Teenager does not work without hi-tech gadgetry. Literally. Specifically, the Teenager does not work without their mobile phone. Half of all Teenagers send more than 50 texts a day, not to mention picture sharing, social networking, games and so on. Digital communication is not just prevalent in Teenagers' lives: it IS Teenagers' lives.

You may think the word 'phone' suggests a machine designed for voice telecommunications. You are wrong because you are a square. The one thing the Teenager almost never does on their phone is call someone. When they do, they're probably:

a) Calling you, their parents
b) Not where they said they'd be
c) Need picking up
d) Not at all bothered by how much this inconveniences you

The Teenager would rather give up a kidney than their mobile phone, and cannot comprehend how you managed to communicate with your friends when you were teenagers. You wrote letters? Letters?

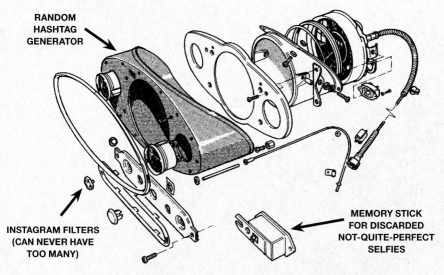

RANDOM HASHTAG GENERATOR

INSTAGRAM FILTERS (CAN NEVER HAVE TOO MANY)

MEMORY STICK FOR DISCARDED NOT-QUITE-PERFECT SELFIES

FIG 2•13 **TEENAGE SOCIAL MEDIA INTERFACE – DECONSTRUCTION**

Ten Commandments of 'Teen Tech'

1) The Teenager must follow fewer people than follow them. This surely defies the laws of maths if taken to its logical extreme, but never mind.

2) The Teenager must comment on and like others' posts. Those who lurk silent in the wings are known as 'ghosts', and being a ghost is no better on social media than it is in *Hamlet*. But the Teenager must not like something too soon after it's posted. A few minutes is good. A few seconds is desperate.

3) The Teenager must time their posts for optimal like-getting – i.e. during post-school social media rush hour. They should remove posts that don't get enough likes.

4) The Teenager must not over-post. One great tweet or pic is worth a dozen mediocre ones. If a photo is not good enough for Snapchat, it should be put on Facebook.

5) The Teenager who posts a selfie must tag their best friends. No, they're not in the photo. Yes, this is a rule. No, there's no logical reason. Yes, because they're Teenagers.

6) The Teenager who wishes to post something they're unsure about should post it privately and tag their friends, who'll advise whether to go ahead or not.

7) The Instagram magic number is 11 (10 likes or fewer are shown by names, but once at 11 it just gives the total).

8) #Whatever #the #Teenager #does #they #shouldn't #over #hashtag.

9) Earbuds are better than full-size headphones in class, as with one bud in and one out the Teenager can listen to music and hear the teacher.

10) Any IT teacher worth their salt will have taught the Teenager well enough to get round the firewall they installed in the first place.

To punish your Teenager take them on holiday to a remote rural cottage where there is no mobile reception or broadband.

Under the influence

Trying to stop Teenagers drinking and taking drugs is rather like trying to nail jelly to the wall. They do it for lots of reasons, but prime among them will be the fact that you don't approve of it.

Adult drinking is Merlot at a dinner party discussing house prices and immigration. Teenage drinking is White Lightning and Malibu in a field putting the world to rights and snogging. One is a lot more fun than the other.

Sooner or later the Teenager will overdo it, and with too much alcohol what goes down must also come up again. The kneeling over the nearest toilet is known as driving the white bus, accompanied by the four onomatopoeic passengers: Huey, Ralph and Bob for those short, sharp alimentary contractions, and Charles, said with extended vowel and a low moan while clinging onto the porcelain once it's all over.

If your Teenager continues to drink, they will suffer some or all of the following: hangovers, memory blanks, impaired judgement, unexplained injuries and sexual malfunction. This should be discouraged, as it is strictly the preserve of the middle-aged. Find your own problems, you upstart teenage brats.

SIX DIFFERENT SPIRITS + LEMONADE

SPINNING STICK TO SELECT NEXT DRINKER

BATH PLUG, BECAUSE A TRAFFIC CONE WOULDN'T FIT.

THERMOMETER, TO RISK MERCURY POISONING

FIG 2•14 **TEENAGE ALCOHOL CONCOCTION**

The average 17-year-old today drinks twice as much as they did ten years ago. Though in fairness they were only 7 ten years ago.

Teenagers and drugs

Drugs have more names than an online petition against Piers Morgan. When the Teenager makes frequent reference to Charlie and Mary Jane, they may not be discussing their new classmates. Similarly:

a) Grass is not always what they play football on.

b) Horse is not always for riding.

c) Brown sugar is not necessarily better for you than white sugar.

d) Snow and rock have little to do with mountaineering.

e) Skunk is not a malodorous black and white mammal.

No teenage group is complete without the self-styled Authority On Drugs™. He (he is almost always a he) usually has a mate, or maybe a mate of a mate, or perhaps he just knows a geezer alright? The Authority On Drugs™ knows everything there is to know about drugs. He knows what's addictive and what's not. He knows what's legal and what's not. He knows this guy who got busted by the pigs, yeah? Of course, what the Authority On Drugs™ really knows is nothing. One of the qualifications for being The Authority On Drugs™ is never admitting that you have no qualifications for being The Authority On Drugs™.

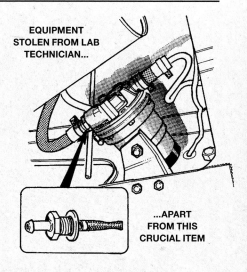

EQUIPMENT STOLEN FROM LAB TECHNICIAN...

...APART FROM THIS CRUCIAL ITEM

FIG 2•15 **BREAKING BAD TEENAGE-STYLE: TRYING TO MAKE DRUGS IN CHEMISTRY GCSE**

WARNING

There are several signs that the Teenager may be using drugs. They may have red eyes and complain of feeling tired all the time. They may show little interest in school. They may be secretive around you. Unfortunately, all these signs are also consistent with Being A Teenager, for which there is no known cure other than time.

Full model range

Teenagers come in several different model ranges. Here are some of the most common:

1. Jocks

Jocks are easily distinguished by the smell of Deep Heat and their insistence on arm-punching their friends by way of greeting. They are hearty and hale, and enjoy nothing more than running around a muddy field on a winter afternoon while equally hearty and hale Teenagers in differently-coloured shirts try to break their legs (football), necks (rugby) or nose (hockey).

2. Geeks

Geeks are usually obsessed with maths and/or computers. They can code as naturally and easily as breathing, and they care little for fashion. They hang out mainly with other geeks and may find themselves the butt of non-geeks' jokes. Teenagers who choose to bully geeks should remember the adage 'the geek shall inherit the earth'. At school reunions in 20 years' time, the geek whose locker was repeatedly destroyed will be driving a Ferrari and running his own hedge fund. He will remember his tormentors, and will delight in asking them how their careers on the Tesco night shift are progressing.

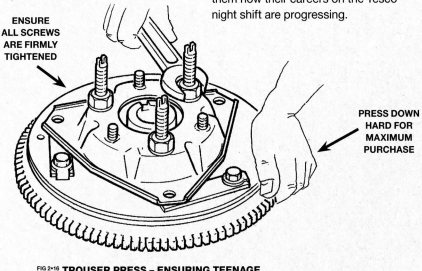

ENSURE ALL SCREWS ARE FIRMLY TIGHTENED

PRESS DOWN HARD FOR MAXIMUM PURCHASE

FIG 2•16 **TROUSER PRESS – ENSURING TEENAGE JEANS ARE AS SKINNY AS POSSIBLE**

3. Skaters

Skaters have stolen the long hair and slacker look of surfers, maybe in revenge for living nowhere near the sea. They wear retro trainers and oversized T-shirts. They call everyone 'dude', which is useful for the Teenager who isn't very good with names. Though they may look rough, they are often too busy actually skateboarding and practising tricks to cause much trouble.

4. Young fogey

Young fogeys dress like people twice their age, which from an adult point of view falls equidistant between the three poles of Comfort, Flattery and Alarm. They are the only people on the planet between the ages of 13 and 18 who tuck their shirts in, and they have rarely seen a heavy tweed waistcoat or antique smoking jacket they didn't like.

5. Emo kids

Emo kids mash up the goth and punk subcultures of yesteryear – both gloomy and rebellious. Like Henry Ford and his paint scheme, they dress in any colour as long as it's black. Unlike Henry Ford, they also go for streaked hair, tattoos and piercings. They are like teenage angst made real, and listen to music that even Ingmar Bergman would have found depressing.

Further variations

Hipsters

The only thing worse than adult hipsters is teenage hipsters. They can't grow proper beards nor afford a £7 bowl of Peruvian muesli.

Scenesters

Close cousin of the hipsters. Hipsters see themselves as more intelligent and cultured. Scenesters see themselves as more trendy and in tune with the zeitgeist. Those not sure of the difference should play safe by giving them all a wide berth.

Nerds

Where geeks obsess about certain things and create cultures around those, nerds are quieter, shyer and more withdrawn.

Young fogies are likely to end up as merchant bankers and therefore be either the only people able to afford basic accommodation or first up against the wall when the revolution comes.

The horn

Teenagerdom lasts for seven years, and in that time the Teenager only thinks about sex twice: once for three years and once for four. Every Teenager talks about it, no Teenager really knows how to do it properly, everyone thinks everyone else is doing it, so everyone claims they are doing it.

Music, technology and fashion all change from one generation of Teenagers to the next, but The Dance Of Ten Thousand Hormones remains constant. There's a reason that you, father of a Teenager XX, are so suspicious of her suitors, and that's

The best way to ensure that Teenager XX's boyfriends are properly vetted is to become President of the United States.

because you were just like they were once. You knows their tactics and their tricks. Heck, if she wasn't your daughter, you might even give them a few tips. But she is your daughter, so if any of those chancers touch a hair on her head you're going to shoot them. After torturing, disembowelling and eviscerating them, obviously.

The relationship

When the Teenager first falls in love, they are convinced that this is a passion so pure and intense as to make Romeo and Juliet look like Terry and June. No-one else – certainly no boring black-hearted bitter parent – can possibly understand. This phase usually lasts three weeks, at best, as indeed does the relationship. Recriminations, drama, taking of sides, switching of sides, gossip and I-can't-believe-they-said-thats usually last 7.5 times as long as the initial relationship.

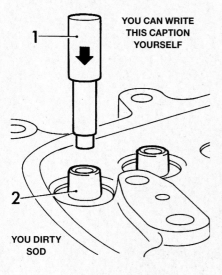

1 — YOU CAN WRITE THIS CAPTION YOURSELF

2 — YOU DIRTY SOD

FIG 2•17 **PARTS COMPATIBILITY**

⚠ **The sex talk**

At some point the parent must have the Sex Talk with the Teenager. This is an occasion that causes untold amounts of dread, embarrassment, sweaty palms, shallow breathing, stomach nerves and a general desire to be anywhere else. The Teenager doesn't enjoy it much either.

The Sex Talk is one of the few dialogues you'll have where the Teenager won't do much answering back. This is not because they agree with you or have been struck dumb by what they perceive as your newfound wisdom. It's because they want the earth to swallow them up or you to leave the room, whichever comes sooner, and they figure that the less they say the quicker it'll be over.

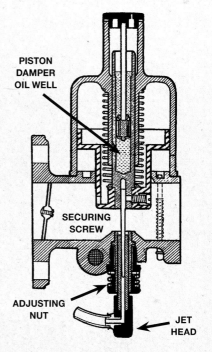

FIG 2•18 **A GOOD DIAGRAM SHOULD MAKE THINGS CLEARER**

Essential DOs and DON'Ts

✓ **DO** say 'your mother and I are concerned, and we think this is an issue worth discussing....'

✓ **DO** keep up to date with the latest sex education and birth-control methods.

✓ **DO** think of this as an ongoing conversation rather than an awkward one-off.

✗ **DON'T** say 'your mother and I still do it, you know. We do. Just the other night, in fact...'

✗ **DON'T** use Powerpoint, flip charts, overhead projectors, graphs or diagrams.

✗ **DON'T** at any stage play Salt n' Pepa's 'Let's Talk About Sex.'

27

Garaging

In 2002–3, Hans Blix and his team of UN inspectors spent several months in Iraq searching for biological and chemical weapons of mass destruction. They found none. It turns out they were looking in the wrong place. Had they searched the average Teenager XY's bedroom (Teenager XX's bedroom of course being full exclusively of sugar and spice and all things nice), they would have located strains of pathogens beyond the ken of all current science. Most items in a Teenager XY's bedroom have a half-life and can only be made safe by being buried under several hundred metres of lead and concrete.

The system
The Teenager will explain away the unholy mess by explaining there is a 'system' and they know where everything is. This is a lie. **There is no system.** Murmurations of starlings have a system. Smoke particles in Brownian motion studies have a system. The Teenager's bedroom has no system.

Even chaos theory has a system. The Teenager's bedroom has no system.

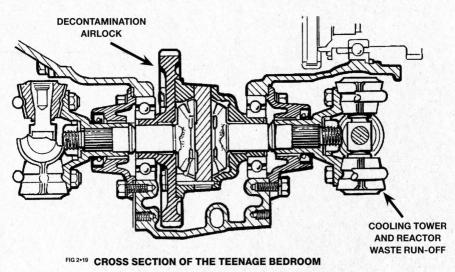

DECONTAMINATION AIRLOCK

COOLING TOWER AND REACTOR WASTE RUN-OFF

FIG 2•19 **CROSS SECTION OF THE TEENAGE BEDROOM**

Enter at your own risk

The Teenager enjoins against all unauthorised entry into their bedroom on pain of – well, that is rarely specified. That no one in their right mind would enter without first donning a full biohazard suit rarely occurs to the Teenager. The Teenager regards unwashed clothes as a helpful layer between the carpet and wherever feet may tread. Teenager XY specimens have been known to:

1) Arrange the contents of their nasal cavity in neat lines across the headboard of their bed, sometimes with helpful annotations ('4th June. Greenie/grey, quite stringy. 7/10').

2) Use Pringles tubes for temporary toiletry purposes. Sometimes they even (a) eat all the Pringles first (b) remember to put the lid back on.

3) Hide contraband in places even a narc cop and his sniffer dog might miss.

4) Use a sock for purposes other than keeping their feet warm.

5) Leave uneaten pizza slices until they've turned hard and grey.

6) Store used condoms in an old Scalextric box.

7) Store decomposing frogs in tupperware containers under the bed, together with logbook detailing time and date of discovery.

8) Pack fireworks into a drawer and then throw a lit match in 'just to see what happens'.

The last method may be the only way of effectively sterilising a Teenager XY's bedroom without calling in the squads who go into nuclear power stations after meltdowns or earthquakes.

WARNING

Proceed with caution.
If possible, first identify major items of furniture – bed, desk, chair – and orientate yourself from there. Do not assume that any towers of magazines, clothes, boxes etc. are inherently stable. One false move and your corpse will be seen on one of those satellite channel programmes about domestic accidents.

Expenditure schedule

The Teenager is expensive, even when it spends much of its time in the garage. In order to minimise and regulate capital outlay on the Teenager, a budget is essential.

Budgeting

Agree both on a monthly sum and the items covered in that sum – bus fares, clothes, toiletries and so on. The amount may seem eye-watering to begin with, but it will almost

GENTLE DRIP-DRIP-DRIP EFFECT

SUBSTANTIAL LEAK SUBSEQUENTLY FIRMLY PLUGGED

FIG 2•20 **DRAINING THE BANK OF MUM AND DAD**

certainly work out cheaper than the drip-drip of 'can I have a tenner to go to the pics?....I need a fiver for the swimming pool…. But everyone's going out tonight and I have to pay my way…'.

The Teenager is unlikely to get the hang of budgeting straight away (if they do, get down the bookies sharpish and put a tenner on them becoming Chancellor of the Exchequer one day – or, given the state of the national finances, maybe not). Sooner rather than later they will have spent their month's money but still want an item. They will ask you nicely. Then they will ask you not so nicely. Then they will tell you they hate you. They will feel they can pester and sulk and tantrum longer than you can. Resist. Do not give in. If you do, you will only foster the buy-now pay-later philosophy that should remain the province of adults, central banks, and Greece.

Teenagers can top up their allowance by doing paid work. The Teenager may tell you they're too busy to go and get a job. This is almost always arrant rubbish.

Teenage jobs

Job	Key skills
Animal shelter	Liking animals. Duh.
Arts and crafts stall	Dexterity to use Stanley knife without injury
Babysitting	Knowing people with children
Bookshop assistant	Basic literacy
Carwashing	Soap and detergent – not a natural teenage fit
Chimney sweep	Time travel back to 1850
Cinema usher	Liking free popcorn
Coffee shop	Encyclopaedic knowledge of latte variations
Department store	Unfazed by general public's rudeness
Dog walking	Natural authority over canines
Errand runner	Good with old dears
Gardening	Green fingers
Golf caddy	Tolerance for men in loud trousers
Hairdressers	Sweeping hair off floor
Life guard	Knowledge of *Baywatch* box set
Local pub	Serving your own parents with a smile
Milk round	Finding the last remaining milkman in Britain
Office intern	Making tea
Paper round	Ability to throw on the move
Pizza delivery	Not looking like a wally on a moped
Sports coaching	Not having two left feet
Tutoring	Actually knowing something about the subject
Waiter/waitress	Showing off by not writing orders down
Warehouse	Ability to enter fugue state
Window cleaning	Lack of vertigo

Redlining the Teenager

As a rule of thumb, the following things will embarrass your Teenager:

a) everything you do
b) everything you don't do
c) your very existence.

Since nothing can rectify this state of affairs, you may as well have some fun in the process.

The extent to which you will embarrass your Teenager is in direct proportion to the enjoyment you will gain from said process. Life as a parent is short enough on joy as it is. Best to take your pleasures where you find them.

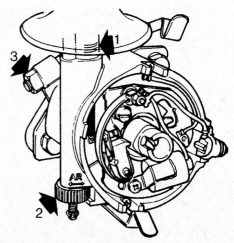

FIG 2•21 **REMEMBER TO PRESS BUTTONS IN THE CORRECT ORDER**

⚠ Measuring embarrassment

Common or garden embarrassment ➤ ➤

Asking too many questions of restaurant staff. Requesting a knife and fork in McDonald's. Calculating the service charge to three decimal places.	Calling them by their childhood nickname. When they cringe and hiss 'shut UP', feign innocence and say: 'what? You love that nickname, don't you?'	Parking too near school. Many Olympians were forged by their insistence on an excessive Parental Vehicle Exclusion Zone and the consequent need to run five miles every day.	Sending your Teenager a friend request on Facebook. When they reject it, sending another. When they block you, asking them why – on Instagram.

Longevity

Most vehicles on the market run better when they're new, and require ever more careful maintenance as they age. The Teenager is the opposite. After seven years of failing to start in the morning, overheating and breaking down without any apparent reason and going either too fast or not at all, the most extraordinary thing happens: the Teenager reaches the grand old age of 20, and suddenly it runs smoothly and calmly.

One year later, at 21, the now ex-Teenager is legally able to do everything not explicitly forbidden in law (though the thought of them flying a plane or driving an HGV will still almost certainly frighten the bejesus out of you).

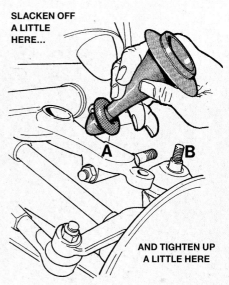

SLACKEN OFF A LITTLE HERE...

A B

AND TIGHTEN UP A LITTLE HERE

FIG 2•22 **FINE TUNING YOUR TEENAGER**

◄   ◄   **Warp the space-time continuum embarrassment**

Bringing out the baby album when their friends come round. Paying special attention to shots of them in the bath, covered in food or falling over.

Trying to be cool by using their slang or aping their dress sense. If you think low-riding jeans look bad on a 16-year-old, rest assured they look much, much worse on a 46-year-old.

Hugging them in public. Taking their panicked 'eww, gross' as a sign to hug them harder, ruffle their hair, and perhaps crack a couple of Tommy Cooper-style gags too.

Dad dancing, of course. Best done with ass shaking, awkward arm movements and singing. Maybe even rapping. Yes, especially with rapping.

Fault diagnosis

Fault	Diagnosis	Treatment
Truculence, stroppiness and general lack of co-operation.	Incurable condition – *Teenagerus maximus*.	The only cure is time. Wait till they're 20 and the situation will magically resolve itself.
Knows everything about everything. Accuses parents of knowing nothing about nothing.	Incurable condition – *Teenagerus maximus*.	The only cure is time. Wait till they're 20 and the situation will magically resolve itself.
Atrocious personal hygiene. Barely tolerates water, draws the line at soap.	Incurable condition – *Teenagerus maximus*.	The only cure is time. Wait till they're 20 and the situation will magically resolve itself.
Plays nothing but ghastly music at piledriver volume.	Incurable condition – *Teenagerus maximus*.	The only cure is time. Wait till they're 20 and the situation will magically resolve itself.
Lies in bed at least till past noon and often till teatime.	Incurable condition – *Teenagerus maximus*.	The only cure is time. Wait till they're 20 and the situation will magically resolve itself.
Speaks bizarre incomprehensible patois.	Incurable condition – *Teenagerus maximus*.	The only cure is time. Wait till they're 20 and the situation will magically resolve itself.
Has terrible mood swings and everything is **SUCH A DRAMA.**	Incurable condition – *Teenagerus maximus*.	The only cure is time. Wait till they're 20 and the situation will magically resolve itself.
Obsessed with sex.	Incurable condition – *Teenagerus maximus*.	The only cure is time. But this won't magically resolve itself at 20. This will go on till about 70.
Obsessed with their phone, of which they never let go.	Incurable condition – *Teenagerus maximus*.	The only cure is time. But this won't magically resolve itself at 20. This will go on till about 70.
Drinking too much.	Incurable condition – *Teenagerus maximus*.	The only cure is time. But this won't magically resolve itself at 20. This will go on till about 70.

Conclusion

So – congratulations! You have survived the Teenager. Wartime gallantry medals have been awarded for less. In time the ex-Teenager will realise what it was like for you in those seven years, and that you weren't lying when you said a thousand times 'you'll understand when you're older'. They'll understand that everything you did came from the same two places – love for them (even when they were being revolting) and fear of them messing up. They'll understand how you had to try and pass on every life lesson you've ever learnt in the tiny window between them being old enough to understand and old enough not to listen.

And in truth, the Teenager is not all bad. Far from it. The Teenager can actually be rather amazing. The Teenager is idealistic and honestly believes they can change the world. The Teenager has energy and optimism and dreams. The Teenager isn't yet bitter or cynical, no matter how much they affect to be. The Teenager reaches for the stars. The Teenager is what we used to be before we shed that adolescent snakeskin in favour of being an adult, and in leaving behind all that angst and shouty music and dodgy clothes, we also left behind a lot of the best things about being human in favour of jobs and mortgages and credit cards.

We were all Teenagers once. And one day your Teenagers will be parents and have Teenagers of their own, and you will be able to watch the process at one remove while enjoying the prerogative of grandparents throughout the ages – the freedom to laugh your arse off at history repeating.

There is much debate about the best moments in life. Your wedding day, the birth of your children, the phone call to say you landed your dream job… They're all great, but there is no moment more precious than hearing your own child, now middle-aged and a frazzled parent, say to their Teenager the six most hated words in the Teenage lexicon:

'Because I said so, that's why.'

Remember that David Bowie was right. Teenagers are quite aware of what they're going through as they try to change their worlds. And the best thing you can do is be there for them when they emerge.

Titles in the Haynes Explains series

001 Babies   ISBN 978 1 78521 102 7

002 Teenagers   ISBN 978 1 78521 103 4

003 Marriage   ISBN 978 1 78521 104 1

004 Pensioners   ISBN 978 1 78521 105 8

Now that Haynes has explained Teenagers, you can progress to our full size manuals on car maintenance (easier and cheaper than maintaining a teenager), *Chieftain Tank Manual* (to fight those battles), *Wine Manual* (from whine to wine) and *Zombie Survival Manual* (say no more).

There are Haynes manuals on just about everything – but let us know if we've missed one.

Haynes.com